On pages 76-79 of *Panzerwrecks 2* we showed a number of Panther Ausf.Ds from Pz.Ers. u. Ausb.Abt.35 knocked out in Bamberg, Germany during April 1945. We think that this is another example based upon the style and location of the Balkenkreuz on the turret side and between the exhausts. The 'Zimmerit' coating on the tank is in excellent condition and shows no signs of prolonged combat, although the right stowage bin has taken a battering. In front of the fence is a tattered seat presumably originating from the tank. Those with an eye for detail will have spotted the emblem on the left stowage bin of a skull on a dark background.

W.Auerbach

Up close and personal with a Sturmgeschütz III Ausf.D, an unusual sight in 1945. Like some other wrecks in this book, it probably belonged to a training unit thrown into battle to stop the Allies. The vehicle has a cylindrical 'Filzbalgvorschaltluftfilter' (pre-filter) on the track guard, next to the air intake; these were fitted to vehicles destined for Greece, Southern Russia and North Africa. Note the different camouflage patterns on the side of the fighting compartment and above the roadwheels.

W.Auerbach

A more complete view of the Sturmgeschütz shows that whoever painted it has gone to a lot of trouble to apply camouflage paint to the area above the roadwheels. The object poking out of the gun barrel is probably the base of a 7.5cm shell.

W.Auerbach

A second series Panzerjäger I with seven-sided superstructure is a another unusual sight in 1945. We have no location or date on the photos but they were probably from the same training and replacement unit as the Panther and Sturmgeschütz. It is unmodified from those examples seen in the early war years apart from a somewhat oversized Balkenkreuz and the missing armoured cover for the exhaust outlet. On page 4 the GI graphically demonstrates the small size of the Panzerjäger.

2x W.Auerbach

The side of the Panzerjäger I shows the tactical number '222'. A 4.7cm shell leans next to the driver's visor, the Panzerjäger could carry a total of 84 rounds of 4.7cm ammunition. Wire has been looped through the tie-downs at the top of the sides of the fighting compartment and hold tree branches that augment the plain Dunkelgelb (RAL 7028) camouflage. The photos on pages 1-6 were taken by a veteran of the US 9th Armored Division who passed across the bridge at Remagen.

W. Auerbach

Pvt. Loy. E. Westbrook of 92nd Cavalry Reconnaissance Squadron, 12th Armored Division photographed a buddy with this knocked out Panther Ausf.G. On the back of the photo he wrote, "This is a German Tiger tank. It took three hits from a '75' and 14 bazookas to knock it out. The crew of five are still inside roasted." The spare roadwheel fitted to the rear side of the turret with the convex side out and track hanger style on the turret are typical of a vehicle belonging to I./Pz.Rgt.15, 11.Panzer-Division.

G.Westbrook

Panzerjäger and Flakpanzers of Meppen

A photographer with the Polish 1. Dywizji Pancernej (1st Armoured Division) caught these Panzerjäger side by side in a vehicle dump in Meppen at war's end. The Pz.Sfl.2 für 7.62cm Pak 36 (Sd.Kfz.132) on the left, with its thin armour and high profile, stands in stark contrast to the heavy 'Jagdpanther' on the right, but both main guns were extremely effective against allied armour. This Jadgpanther was seen in *Panzerwrecks 3*, page 93, and has the sectional gun tube and single driver's pivotable periscope. It appears to have a very late war modification as well: additional armour shields over the engine air intake and exhaust louvres. Other details are obscured by heavy camouflage. **PISM**

The low slung menace of two Panzer IV/70(V)s and a Jagdpanzer IV show the evolution of the Panzer IV into a formidable tank killer. The vehicle on the right appears to have more than 20 kill-rings on its barrel. The tactical number on the Jagdpanther is obscured by another gun barrel, but the Jagdpanther probably belonged to 2/s.H.Pz.Jg.Abt 655. As well, it has the four bolt drive sprocket/hub combination seldom seen on these vehicles.

PISM

A 'doctored' photo of a well known Jagdpanther (see inset photo on page 11. Our apologies to our readers, but the General was just too distracting, and the bit of roof detail lost was minimal.) We are beginning to see more of the vehicles that first appeared in *Panzerwrecks 3*. This may be the fourth vehicle in from the right on page 92 if the hole in the front portion of the mudguard matches, although the headlamp shown here has come apart. Note the 'T' shaped 'key' on the roof hatch. The Panzer IV/70(V) with tactical number '322' no doubt belongs to 3./s.H.Pz.Jg.Abt.655.

LAC

The same Jagdpanther with its camouflage net pulled down to reveal its stripes. No tactical numbers are evident, only a small Balkenkreuz. What is very evident is the additional armour over the right cooling air intake louvre! Next to the Jagdpanther is an early Sturmgeschütz III, possibly from Pz.Einsatz.Abt.20. In the background, all manner of self propelled Flak vehicles are neatly lined up.

PISM

Panzerjäger and Flakpanzers of Meppen

Several 3.7cm Flak 43/1 auf Selbstfahrlafette (s.W.S.), both armoured and unarmoured, are lined up next to 2cm Flakvierling 38 auf Selbstfahrlafette (Sd.Kfz.7/1). From available photographs, it appears the s.W.S. was prone to front axle/wheel troubles. Both unarmoured s.W.S. have "Cdn War Museum" on the fenders. Capital letters (F, G, etc) appear on the inside of the uppermost portion of the gun shield that elevates with the gun. The drop side panel of the nearest vehicle has been repaired with unpainted wood. Next to it is a pedestal mount (Fliegerabwehr-Sockellafette) for four 7.92 mm M.G.17 or a single M.G. 151, etc. Those wishing a insightful view as to how enemy AFVs and assorted weaponry were herded back to Canada would do well to read 'My Father's Son - Memories of War and Peace', by Farley Mowat, who served as IO [Tech] Material for the Canadians in WW2.

PISM

A closer view of the vehicle on page 12 with the sides of the fighting platform lowered shows the immense size of the 3.7cm Flak 43/1 and the need to provide working space for five Kanoniere to service the quick firing weapon (the design featured a new gas operated breech mechanism). The ammo compartments at the very rear appear to be missing. To the left, on the armoured version, we can see the canvas tilt that protected the crew seats. In the foreground, a 3.7cm Flak 36 minus its barrel and an unidentified trailer, purpose unknown.

PISM

Above: A distant photo reveals an even more extensive line up of AFVs, including a rare 'Möbelwagen'. **Below**: Two 2cm Flakvierling 38 auf Selbstfahrlafette (Sd.Kfz.7/1), and two 2cm Flak 38 auf Selbstfahrlafette (Sd.Kfz.10/5) sandwich two Drilling mounts on a trailer, a very makeshift solution to AA protection. The Drillings are the Luftwaffe mounts, with padded shoulder yokes.
1x PISM, 1x LAC

This is the Möbelwagen seen on the far left of the photo on page 14. It was taken at the Eclipse dump in Oldenburg before being moved to Meppen. A rear view of the Flakpanzer also appears on page 55 of *Panzerwrecks 2*. The front armoured shield has a cut out to allow the gun to be used in the ground role while offering the crew some protection. The idler here is the later cast type, whereas the photo in *Panzerwrecks 2* shows an earlier welded type on the other side. The Flakpanzer almost definitely belonged to s.H.Pz.Jg.Abt. 655. Note the opened pistol port on the side of the superstructure an what appears to be a baby duck emblem on the front.

Archive of Modern Conflict - R381-01

In *Panzerwrecks 1* we published a photograph of a Panther Ausf.A back-fitted with 'Flammenvernichter' mufflers on the exhausts. Well here is another photographed in Germany in May 1945. Unusually, the mufflers are fixed flat against the rear plate by metal bands. The tank may have been driven without mufflers as there is some staining above the armoured exhaust outlets. It is missing the rear stowage bins like the *Panzerwrecks 1* example, although there is no spare wheel fixed to the turret and the gun cleaning rod tube is mounted in its usual position.

ECPA via C.Gillono

From any other angle the Panther is standard issue. The 'Zimmerit' is in very good condition, as are the mudguards leading us to believe that it was possibly a training vehicle. The tank lacks a tactical number, insignia or camouflage pattern making identification impossible. The photo on page 18 provides an excellent view of the vehicle's opened hatches.

1x Ø.Leonsen, C.Leeman, D.Campbell, D.Parker. 1x ECPA via C.Gillono

Panzer '632' belonged to II./Pz.Rgt.15 of 11.Panzer-Division. The tank, an early Pz.Kpfw.IV Ausf.H, had suffered engine problems and was towed to this location outside Ablis, France. At some time before the German withdrawal on 19 August 1944 it was sabotaged, as is obvious from the spiked gun barrel. With the spare roadwheels gone from their rack we can see how light the paintwork was before dirt, combat and perhaps smoke darkened it.

L.Archer

Visitors pose for a snapshot on the remnants of a StuG M42 mit 75/18 850(i). The paintwork is in fairly good condition indicating that the photo was taken not long after the war. The photograph was bought in Austria, so perhaps this is where it was taken. It is interesting to note that the camouflage paint scheme was applied on the lower hull sides and on the drive sprocket. Useful items such as the roadwheels, return rollers and engine have vanished.

L.Arche

404th Fighter Group		48th Fighter Group	
Airfield Location	Initial OP Date	Airfield Location	Initial OP Date
Chippelle, France	05-Jul-44	Deux Jumeaux, France	30-Jun-44
Bretigny, France	29-Aug-44	Villacoublay, France	30-Aug-44
Juvincourt, France	07-Sep-44	Cambrai/Niergnies, France	12-Sep-44
St.Trond, Belgium	18-Sep-44	St.Trond, Belgium	18-Sep-44
Kelz, Germany	24-Mar-45	Kelz, Germany	24-Mar-45
Fritzlar, Germany	31-Mar-45	Kassel/Rothwesten, Germany	07-Apr-45
		Illesheim, Germany	17-Apr-45

The photos on pages 21-23 are from the same veteran's collection, and all we know was that he was an airman in a USAAF fighter squadron. One of his other photos had 'St Trond' written on the back, which was a location of an airfield home to both the 48th and 404th Fighter Squadrons, but the photos may have been taken anywhere where he was stationed.

(See above.) Based on the method of fixing the spare track hooks on the turret with the cut end welded to the turret sides, this Panther Ausf.G may have belonged to I./Pz.Rgt.24.

W.Auerbach

Two snapshots of a standard production Sturmgeschütz IV immobilised by track problems that have caused them to run off the drive sprockets and pile up in front of the vehicle. The links in the track have the open guide horns whereas the spare links draped on the driver's compartment have solid guide horns.

2x W.Auerbach

4 July 1945, British soldiers look over a Tiger I that has just been fired on by an Archer tank destroyer at the Haustenbeck Proving Grounds in Germany. The Tiger had been immobile, being minus its wheels and tracks. Quite what has sheared off the side armour is unknown, but it gives a unique view of the ammunition racks and the void by the side of the engine compartment that would have housed a fuel tank and part of the cooling system.
4x NARA

A Tiger II at an unknown location. It carries the tactical number '311' on the turret side, although light filtering through the trees makes this difficult to see. Other than the truncated gun, the tank looks to be in fairly good shape; all of the hatches are still in place ruling out an internal explosion. It is likely that the vehicle had to be abandoned and was sabotaged to prevent its re-use. But by whom? The crew, the I-Staffel or the Allies? The long thin tube going from the engine deck to the hull side is a vent for the fuel system. In the background is another Tiger II.

W.Auerbach

A Tiger without claws. This photo taken by S/Sgt. Alde Brekke, a tanker with the 11th Armored Division shows a Tiger II of s.Pz.Abt.506 after the removal or destruction of the gun. As is often the case with 'trophy' photos taken in the field the GI is standing in exactly the wrong place as his legs are covering the first digit of the tactical number. The s.Pz.Abt.506 used a system whereby the first digit was separated from the other two by the Balkenkreuz, making this tank either 1+10, 2+10 or 3+10.

M.Bowers

A 'see through' Jagdtiger somewhere in Germany at the end of the War. An explosion (probably courtesy of the crew setting demolition charges) has blown the great beast apart, leaving just the front and rear armour. It allows a unique view of the how it was put together, most notably the large 'braces' that helped support the glacis plate and the massive cast superstructure front. The cooling system for the engine is visible behind this. The photo on page 30 was taken by Sgt. Oscar Ryg of HQ Company, 20th Armored Infantry Battalion, 10th Armored Division. The photo on this page by Bill Beckett serving in the 63rd Infantry Division. **1x H.Liddic, 1x W.Beckett**

Sušice, Czechoslovakia, May 1945. Two trains laden with wrecks are captured on motion picture film by US Signal Corps cameramen. On the left is a m.S.P.W. (Sd.Kfz.251) minus half of its armour, followed by a pair of m.S.P.W. (7.5cm Pak) (Sd.Kfz.251/22), one being a late production vehicle with rearward hinged engine access hatch. Behind this is a Sturmgeschütz III Ausf.G covered in concrete and without its gun - although the box mantlet remains. The train on the right shows an ISU-122, a late production Pz.Kpfw.IV Ausf.J without the gunner's visor and the bare hull of a Panzer IV/70(V) or Jagdpanzer IV. On page 31 the cameraman has turned 180 degrees revealing an empty ISU-122 engine bay, the bones of a Panther Ausf.G, a Bergepanther and the rear of the Sd.Kfz.251/22 with what appear to be steel capped tracks inside. **4x NARA**

This is the train on the right of page 31. The Sturmgeschütz III Ausf.G in the foreground is very interesting as it is liberally covered in T-34 tracks. These would have been welded onto the sloping front plate; some of the welds can still be seen even though the tracks have gone. Also a ridge is obvious down the middle of the cast 'Topfblende' mantlet, which has an opening for a coaxial M.G. The Pz.Kpfw.IV Ausf.J behind it was one of a number shipped to Hungary between August and December 1944 and has the registration number '5H457' above the driver's visor. It has lifting loops on the top corners of the superstructure and thickened armour on the turret exhaust fan cover. **2x NARA**

Two GIs from the 778th Tank Battalion take turns to pose with a wrecked Sturmgeschütz III Ausf.G in the Hunsrück Mountains during January or February 1945. The tactical number of '514' on the side of the fighting compartment indicates its use by a Panzer-Divison, rather than a StuG Brigade, Infanterie-Division, or Volksgrenadier-Division, all of whom had no more than three companies. The 11.Panzer-Division is known to have possessed a few Sturmgeschütz at this time and with the large black tactical number we think it belonged to 5./Pz.Rgt.15.

2x L.Archer

A Sturmgeschütz III Ausf.G knocked out in Czechoslovakia in 1945. The sign by the drive sprocket reads: "Zničen II. tankovým praporem" (destroyed by 2nd Tank Battalion). On page 74 of *Panzerwrecks 3* we showed a wrecked Panther Ausf.G with a similar sign which was knocked out by the 1st Czech Tank Brigade in northern Moravia, perhaps this Sturmgeschütz was another of their kills? It has unusual 'Schürzen' that cover only the fighting compartment, 'Zimmerit' and a 'Rundumfeuer' M.G. mount on the roof.

VHU

The remains of a Sturmgeschütz photographed by Howard. L. Simon of the US 119th A.A.A. Battalion near Thionville, France in November 1944. Given the date and location, there are two possibilities as to who operated it; Pz.Jg.Abt.1119 of 19.Volksgrenadier-Division (whose second company was equipped with Sturmgeschütz) or Pz.Jg.Abt.25 fighting as a Kampfgruppe 25.Panzergrenadier-Division, with two companies of Sturmgeschütz. The vehicle is a mess; no engine deck, broken tracks and sabotaged gun - or was it a lucky shot?

H.Simon

A Sturmhaubitze 42 photographed in the 'Place d'Armes', but in what town? The circular sign on the background reads 'information and recreation center' adding to the mystery. From this side we can see that the vehicle was outfitted for a 'Rundumfeuer' M.G. mount, although it was not actually fitted, a blanking plate has been bolted on instead. The 10.5cm Sturmhaubitze 42 has the muzzle brake of a Wespe.

W. Auerbach

A GI poses with the vehicle. It has a more or less complete coating of 'Zimmerit', including on the opened brake access hatch, and a very fresh looking Balkenkreuz on the side of the fighting compartment. The front two roadwheels are missing their armoured hubcaps, exposing the bearings. **W.Auerbach**

Panzer Remnants on a Czech Road

It's an idyllic day, and young boys find playing on a flak mount to be irresistible fun. This is an early version of the 2cm Flakvierling 38 auf Selbstfahrlafette (Sd.Kfz.7/1) with the guns on a central rotating base. The emblem on the superstructure is repeated on the rear track guard and indicates the parent unit to be the 6.Panzer-Division (different colours could be used with this emblem to differentiate subunits within the division). The location may be Havlíčkuv Brod or Polna, near Jihlava, Czecholslovakia, two locations where the 6.Pz.Div. operated in the closing days of the war. The side panel to the engine compartment rests on the crew seat.

L.Archer

German and Russian vehicles interspersed along a road in Havlíčkuv Brod could be from anywhere, and underscore the confused final days as units intermingled and permutated to deal with daily exigencies. This gutted mittlerer Schützenpanzerwagen (Sd.Kfz.251), sharing a road with a T-34, gives little information other than an emblem of a unknown unit on its rear plate. The 8.Pz.Div. absorbed elements of Pz.Gren.Btl. Neuhammer and Pz.Gren.Btl. 19/IV Kamenz; all three had m.S.P.W. Note the missing outer roadwheels.
L.Archer

This 'Drilling,' tactical number '444,' carries a clue on its nose armour, the 'die' insignia of 8.Panzer-Division. The last available 'Kriegsgliederung' of the 8.Pz.Div. dated 1.4.45 showed 'Drillinge' only with the 4./Pz.Gren.Rgt.98, however, if all the vehicles on these pages belonged to the Pz.A.A.8, it is possible that the final m.S.P.W. shipment in March included some Sd.Kfz.251/21. This example had the late war engine hatch, and three 'uberschwere' M.G.151 in a low mounting, obviating the need for the auxiliary 'Zusatzpanzerung'.

L.Archer

A heavy recon car, or schwerer Panzerspähwagen (7.5cm) (Sd.Kfz.234/3) presumed to belong to Stabskp./Pz.A.A.8, sits astride a road in Havlíčkuv Brod. This unit received 13 Sd.Kfz.234/1 and 3 Sd.Kfz.234/3 during September 1944 and four additional replacements in March 1945. Based on the tactical number '082' the company may have been divided into eight two-car troops, with a Sd.Kfz.234/1 and a 234/3 paired in 8 Pz.Späh-Trupp. We have no explanation for the eight 'staples' welded to the bow armour or other brackets appearing elsewhere on the vehicle.

L.Archer

Panzer Remnants on a Czech Road

This mittlerer Schützenpanzerwagen (7.5cm Pak) (Sd.Kfz.251/22), with its neatly applied tactical number '442' and camouflage, is another fourth company vehicle in an ad hoc unit. Units were often authorised a certain K.St.N. 'als Anhalt' which meant they were to adopt to that K.St.N. as best as possible with available material. Certainly this unit packed a lot of punch. Note the flat visors, missing outer roadwheels and the bracket for a shovel on the side of the engine compartment. To the rear is a normal m.S.P.W.

L.Archer

Although a better look at the stencil on the side of this m.S.P.W. (7.5cm Pak) (Sd.Kfz.251/22) might tell us if it was a factory produced vehicle or a converted m.S.P.W. (7.5cm Kanone) (Sd.Kfz.251/9), the normal pattern engine deck and the reinforced roof plate with four 'tabs' along the front seem to indicate the latter. Next to it, a 2cm Flak 38 auf Selbstfahrlafette Zgkw.3t (Sd.Kfz.11), minus gun and carriage, carries an inexplicable star on its nose armour. Note the sunken ammo storage compartments in the gun platform and missing side driver's visor.

L.Archer

A hand painted RSO/01, formerly of 19.Volksgrenadier-Division sits at a US motor pool in Sierck-les-Bains, France on 26 November 1944. To the upper and lower right of the divisional insignia is the 'artillerie' tactical marking. This is a KHD built vehicle as corroborated by the enlarged unladen weight of 3700 under the data box on the driver's door. The US captors have added an aircraft recognition panel on the cab roof and careful inspection reveals a US helmet sitting on top of the engine in the cab. A full complement of snow cleats are in the rack on the side of the vehicle. Note the snow chains are fitted to the rear wheels of the Jeep. **US Army**

An RSO/03 brought in from the front by Lt.Col. Richard. D. Sutton of 347th Infantry Regiment, 87th Infantry Division on 13 January 1945 in St. Hubert, Belgium. The original caption states that the unidentified soldier leaning out of the cab is French. The insignia on the front is that of the US 79th Infantry Division. **US Army**

A Jagdpanzer 38 and in the background a pair of Sturmgeschütz III Ausf.G knocked out by 1. Dywizji Pancernej (Polish 1st Armoured Division) in the Netherlands during October/November 1944. The Jagdpanzer is typical of those assembled between May and July 1944, with the original pattern of idler wheels, no heat guard over the exhaust muffler and 'ears' on the gun mount. The towing points of Jagdpanzer 38s are often photographed broken - as we see here. An explosion has blown the hatches open and unseated the 'Schürzen' from their mountings.

PISM

Five Jagdpanzer 38s captured by Czech forces. The number 432/1 on the vehicle in the foreground is a Czech inventory number rather than a tactical number. The second Jagdpanzer has a paint scheme seen on B.M.M. assembled vehicles, the others are painted in the Škoda pattern; note the similarity between the patterns & placement of colours on the Škoda vehicles. There are camouflage loops welded to the fighting compartment sides indicating that the vehicles were manufactured sometime in 1945. Interestingly the Jagdpanzer in the foreground has two sets of tarpaulin tie downs on the sides of the superstructure.

P.Doležal

Two photos, possibly of the same tank from I./Pz.Rgt.3, 2.Panzer-Division, near Celles in Belgium, a casualty of 'Wacht am Rhein'. The diagonal bands of camouflage indicate that the tank was assembled by M.N.H. A few interesting details can be seen on page 51 such as the rear turret hatch is holding open the engine access hatch, the pie-slice sections stowed on top of the 'Kampfraumheizung' (crew compartment heater).

2x TTM

A Panther Ausf.D with two tactical numbers. An older number consisting of a '1' and a '2' are somewhat faded, but thankfully enough of the '176' remains. The style of the tactical number and the fact that it is repeated on the turret rear point to the tank having belonging to Schießschule der Pz.Tr. Putlos, which in turn was assigned to Panzer-Division 'Clausewitz'. The photo was from an album relating to the 11 Royal Tank Regiment.

TTM

A veteran of the early years; a Sturmgeschütz III Ausf.C or D minus its roof is looked over by curious US airmen. In addition to the tactical number '2', there is a Balkenkreuz and the tactical marking for a Sturmgeschütz Kompanie on the side.
Ø.Leonsen, C.Leeman, D.Campbell, D.Parker

The tactical number '2' and Balkenkreuz are repeated on the smoke grenade rack at the rear of the hull. A rail has been fitted to the back of the engine deck so as it may be used for stowage. The airman centre-frame on page 55 has his hand on the starter crank.

Ø.Leonsen, C.Leeman, D.Campbell, D.Parker

Two views of a Panzer.IV/70(A) in the ruined village of Mittelwihr, France on 8 February 1945. The vehicle belonged to 7./Pz.Rgt.2, attached to Panzer-Brigade.106 who fought there in early December 1944. There is evidence of small arms fire on the front armour and the gun mantlet, although the shot though the drive sprocket and into the final drive probably stopped the vehicle. At the very top of the superstructure armour (above the muzzle) is a pure black Balkenkreuz, unlike the regular white outlined examples on the sides. The 'Drahtgeflecht-Schürzen' (wire mesh skirts) are positioned to clear 'Ostketten' should the wider track need to be fitted. **2x US Army**

Left: A GI poses on top of a 'sunken' early production Pz.IV/70(A). This photo has been captioned with what seems to read 'Tegernsee'. We think that the location has been mis-spelt, or is incorrect. According to Martin Block the 17.SS-Pz.Gren.Div. with the I./Pz.Rgt.HG attached started reporting a single 'Jagdpz.IV (Ente)' in their war diary during the first week of May 1945. Could this be what they meant? Or is it more likely that we are looking at a vehicle from Pz.Brig.106 or II./Pz.Rgt.GD as these units fought in the west and were both issued with early vehicles such as we see here with four return rollers and bolted towing points. The vehicle has had loops welded to the top of the gun mount, mantlet, front plate, and unusually, the gun barrel.
W.Auerbach

Right: One for the ladies. A shirtless GI poses in a Pz.Kpfw.Turm II (Normalserie) - Bauform 229 Bugpanzerdach. This bunker used the top deck of a Pz.Kpfw.II in addition to the turret, this example being from an Ausf.F. Note that the inside of the commander's hatch is painted in 'Elfenbein' (ivory) rather than the external colour. **L.Archer**

Winter style. Two infantrymen from the 114th Infantry Regiment of the 44th Infantry Division dressed in the US Army's latest white camouflage covering, stand in front of an abandoned Flammpanzer 38 from Panzer-Flamm-Kompanie.353 in the town of Gros-Réderching, France on 13 January 1945. A thin covering of snow obscures the factory applied camouflage scheme.

US Army

Another Flammpanzer 38 in Gros-Réderching, this one well known. Pfc. Thomas Tully and Pvt. George Bates of the 114th Infantry Regiment, 44th Infantry Division check out the snow covered vehicle. Twenty B.M.M. built Jagdpanzer 38 were converted to Flammpanzer in December 1944. This one has spare tracks in a rack welded to the side of the superstructure.

US Army

Flammpanzer 'S14' was captured in Gros-Réderching, France in January 1945. At the request of the US Army it was towed to Oermingen, some 12km to the South West by the French 2DB on 10 January 1945 and a detailed report was made by the Chemical Officer of the US 7th Army on 12 January. The US report states, "A smoke ejector was located over the right rear fender." This photo shows the fender but seems to show only jack mounts, so is this mysterious bracket for a smoke discharger? At the rear of the vehicle, below the 'Flammenvernichter', is the exhaust and muffler for the D.K.W. flame oil pump

TTM

The Flammpanzer 38 lacks the nose-heaviness of the Jagdpanzer 38. The roof of the Flammpanzer differs in details such as having a handle in front of the 'Rundumfeuer' M.G.34 mount, indicating the presence of a hatch, an arch-shaped object at the front of the roof and the bracket over the 'Flammenvernichter' exhaust on the engine deck.

US Army

The front of 'S14'. Here we can see that the vehicle is not one of the examples on page 60 or 61 as there differences in the camouflage pattern and front mudguards. It is not unusual to see a Flammpanzer 38, or Jagdpanzer 38, minus one or both of its towing points as they tended to shear off as seen here. The object above the flamethrower is the operator's periscope, behind this is the armour of the M.G. mount. This was in a different position compared to a Jagdpanzer 38 and according to the US report was "mounted behind the hatch and approximately equidistant from the front, rear and sides of the tank". The low height of the vehicle is obvious against the GI.

US Army

The flamethrower without its sheet metal shield. In the background on the roof is an opened crew hatch and the 'Rundumfeuer' M.G. mount. According to the report the gun had the appearance of a 5inch howitzer from a distance. **Inset:** a drawing of the shield from the report.
2x US Army

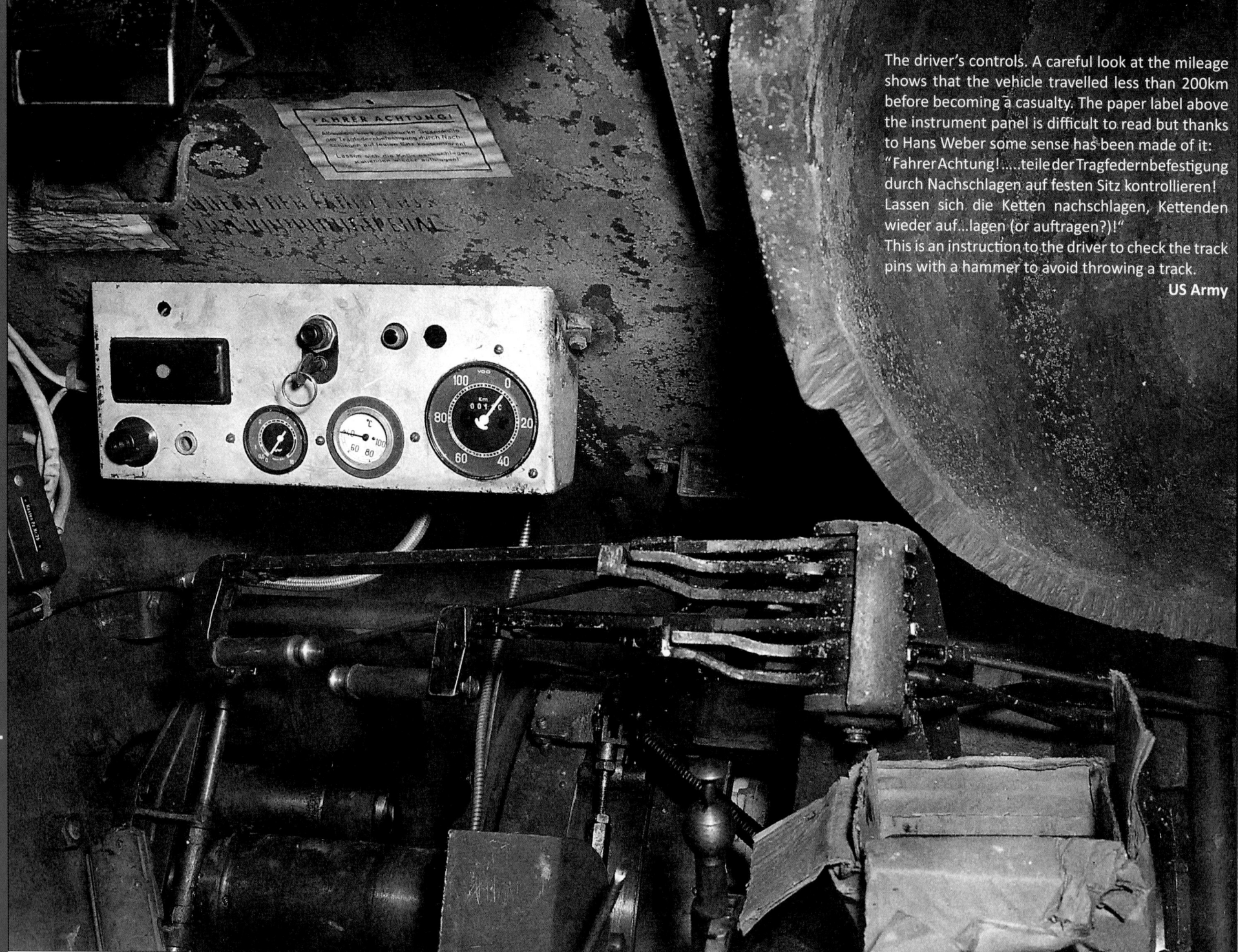

The driver's controls. A careful look at the mileage shows that the vehicle travelled less than 200km before becoming a casualty. The paper label above the instrument panel is difficult to read but thanks to Hans Weber some sense has been made of it: "Fahrer Achtung! ....teile der Tragfedernbefestigung durch Nachschlagen auf festen Sitz kontrollieren! Lassen sich die Ketten nachschlagen, Kettenden wieder auf...lagen (or auftragen?)!"
This is an instruction to the driver to check the track pins with a hammer to avoid throwing a track.

US Army

The flamethrower operator's position. The left handle controls elevation and traverse and the right handle fires the weapon. The report states "that the gun is pivoted from two light metal straps," which must be the ones in front of the periscope. It goes on to say that the weapon had an approximate elevation of -5 to +35 degrees and a traverse of 20 degrees left and 40 degrees right. **US Army**

The left side of the interior showing the driver's seat and top view of the engine and the fuel tank for the flame oil pump. M.G. ammunition and drums litter the floor, along with a periscope. The photographer has dropped part of his 'Kodak' film packaging amidst the detritus too. **US Army**

Looking through the hatch showing the flamethrower operator's seat, and behind it the main tank for the flame oil. Assuming that the 'Pilze' mount seen in the lower left of the photo is on top of the glacis plate above the driver, that would put the placement of the hatch at the front of the roof about half-way between the driver and flamethrower operator. The M.G. mount can be seen behind. Page 71 shows the firewall with empty radio racks and one of the flame oil tanks in the upper right. **2x US Army**

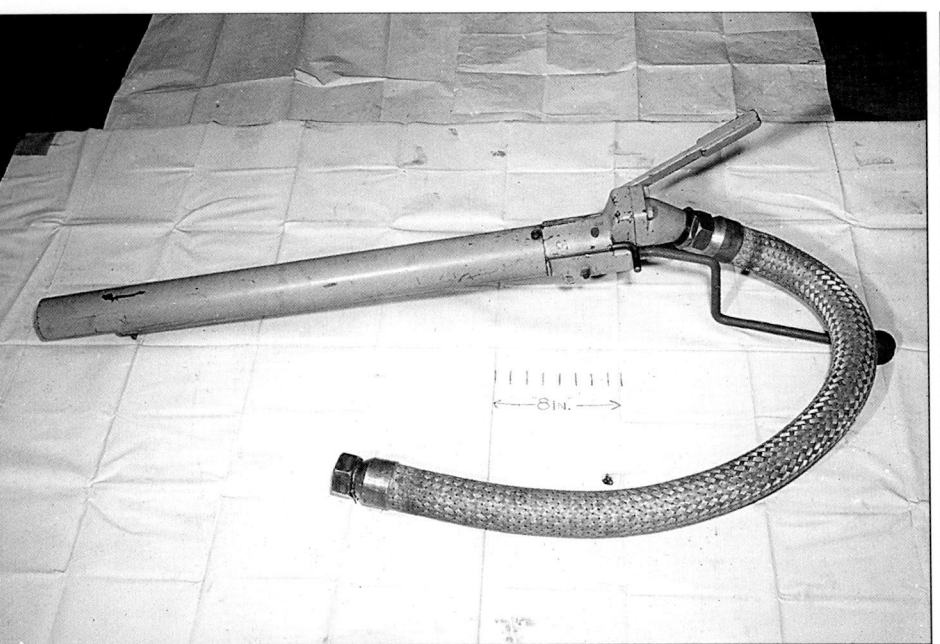

The flamethrower in varying states of disassembly. The report goes on to say: "On depressing the operating lever to the fullest extent, three equally spaced clicks are heard. The first click places a cartridge in firing position. The second click fires the cartridge, and the third click opens the fuel valve. Upon releasing the lever, the fuel valve is closed and the spent or still burning cartridge is ejected."

4x US Army

Karl-Gerät Nr. V 'Loki' as captured by US forces in Germany, March/April 1945 while on its rail transporter. Significant damage has been caused to one of the transporters, peeling back the steelwork. The prominent recoil housing normally seen on top of the gun was dismounted for rail travel.

L.Archer

The massive weapon must have been quite a sight. A tanker from a unit operating M36B1s wrote the following on the back of the photo on page 74: "The German 420mm mortar. The barrel is big enough for a person to get into. June 20 1945 near Altenkirchen". The photograph on this page was taken a little later on July 12. The barrel was actually 540mm. **Inset:** Sgt. O'Brien lying with a shell.

3x L.Archer

The chassis number on the rear plate of 65546 tells us this is a Pz.Kpfw.III Ausf.G built by Alkett. It has a 6b./Z.W. turret armed with a 5cm Kw.K in an external mantlet and older type commander's cupola. We have no location or date for this photo, but it is quite possible, given the age of the tank that it belonged to a training unit. **L.Archer**

Wreckage at the end of the war as photographed by an unknown GI. The Pz.Kpfw.III is a vehicle from a Funklenk unit; Pz.Vers.u.ers.Abt.300(Fkl) as corroborated by the 'PV-421' registration number on the driver's front plate and the armoured box for the extra radio equipment at the rear of the turret. On 3 April 1945 the Pz.Vers.u.ers.Abt.300(Fkl) was disbanded and incorporated into what was left of the 2.Panzer-Division, this may account for the Flakpanzer IV 'Wirbelwind' in the background since none were issued to Pz.Vers.u.ers.Abt.300(Fkl).

L.Archer

A Sd.Kfz.250 with a turret? Sadly not. In fact it is merely a humble le.S.P.W. (2cm) (Sd. Kfz.250/9) Ausf.B being cut up for scrap with an ISU-122S in the background (we know it is a Sd.Kfz.250/9 because other photos show it with the turret). Also in the background is a weaponless 2cm Flak 38 auf Sfl. (Sd.Kfz.10/5). The cutting crew has removed the thin steel stowage bin that ran along the hull side of the Sd.Kfz.250 - this is sitting upside down in the foreground. To the right is a T-34/85 turret, complete with flowers. The photo was taken in the Štitina - Velká Polom area of Czechoslovakia after the war.

VHU

27 December 1944, a s.Pz.Sp.Wg. (5cm) (Sd.Kfz.234/2) and a Zgkw.12t (Sd.Kfz.8) sit in railway sidings after the failure of 'Wacht am Rhein'. The most likely location for the photo is Ciney, Belgium. The Sd.Kfz.234/2 was from Pz.Aufkl.Abt.2 and formed part of 'Kampfgruppe von Böhm', the halftrack shows a towed artillery tactical sign on the rear, probably that of Pz.Art.Rgt.74. The armoured car carries the tactical number '181' on the turret side, with the Truppe number '8' stencilled in white on the forward stowage bin. Vehicles from this unit whose tactical number ended in '1' had the Truppe numbers painted in white, while those ending in '2' were painted in a darker colour, either red or black.

US Army via R.Spezzano

The photos shown here and on page 81 show four Pz.Kpfw.IV from 6./SS-Pz.Rgt.1 that were knocked out in Rocourt, Belgium on the night of 7/8 September 1944 after a run-in with US forces. The main photograph has some embellishments courtesy of the photographer: a 'sign' on the drive sprocket indicating his unit and an inked out area above the idler covering the sign of another unit. **Inset**: Total destruction.

2x R.Kosick

Garden furniture Yank style. A GI poses with a wreck minus its muzzle brake, crew hatches and some turret 'Schürzen' in Rocourt, while the inset photo shows another, headless, example. Recommended further reading about these vehicles are 'Duel in the Mist' by De Meyer, Haasler, MacDougall, Vosters and Weber, and 'Hold the Westwall or perish with it' by Timm Haasler.

2x R.Kosick

Quick Fix: Rocket Firing SPWs

In December, 1944, the US 7th Armored Group assigned to the 30th Infantry Division the task of using a new, untested, weapon system - the 4.5" Rocket Launcher, T-34 - in support of an upcoming infantry assault. Plans called for the 29th Infantry Division to establish a bridgehead over the Roer River in the vicinity of Julich, Germany. The 30th ID was to cross the river behind the 29th and launch an attack to the SE. The zone of the 30th ID included the Staatsforst Hambach, deemed to be an outstanding obstacle with the enemy dug in on the N and W sides of the woods. It was planned, therefore, to saturate these woods with rocket fire just prior to launching the attack. The T-34, nicknamed the 'Calliope,' was a 60 tube launcher capable of firing a 38.5 pound HE rocket out to 2,900 yards, and was designed to fit on the turret of the M4 Medium Tank. Twenty-two launchers were to be mounted on tanks of the 743rd Tank Bn. In addition, the 3508th Ord.Med.Auto.Maint Co was designated to design, construct, and install a suitable mount for the T-34 in five captured German halftracks. Here, a m.S.P.W., tactical number '405,' is being stripped of all interior fittings prior to mounting the launcher.

US Army

Work began on 4 December 1944 and was completed by 9 December. The top carriage of a 7.5cm Pak 40 stood in for the tank turret to provide a mechanism to elevate the launcher. No traverse was possible. Here troops lop off the end of the gun barrel.

3x US Army

Interior of a gutted Sd.Kfz.251/21. Note extended roof armour and gun travel lock. **2x US Army**

Quick Fix: Rocket Firing SPWs

Quick Fix: Rocket Firing SPWs

Work continues on the Sd.Kfz.251/21. The bottom of the 7.5cm Pak carriage was shorn of all parts that protruded to insure a smooth surface, and then it was welded directly to sections of railroad track, 51" long, crosswise in the crew compartment. A slit two feet wide in the armour was made in one side and a three foot wide opening was made in the other. The gun barrel, which had about 3 feet cut off the end, pointed over the right side of the halftrack through the two foot slit. Two pieces of heavy 12" I-beams, approximately 23" long, provided a support to which the launcher trunnions were welded and the equilibrator springs anchored. The driver's compartment was completely enclosed by boiler plate in the rear and an entrance hatch was provided (the hinges from the engine hatches were appropriated for this entrance hatch). At times, the armoured hull was removed to expedite the conversion. The floor plates were also removed, exposing the vehicle's gas tanks and batteries to sparks from the welders. None of the vehicles were runners. **2x US Army**

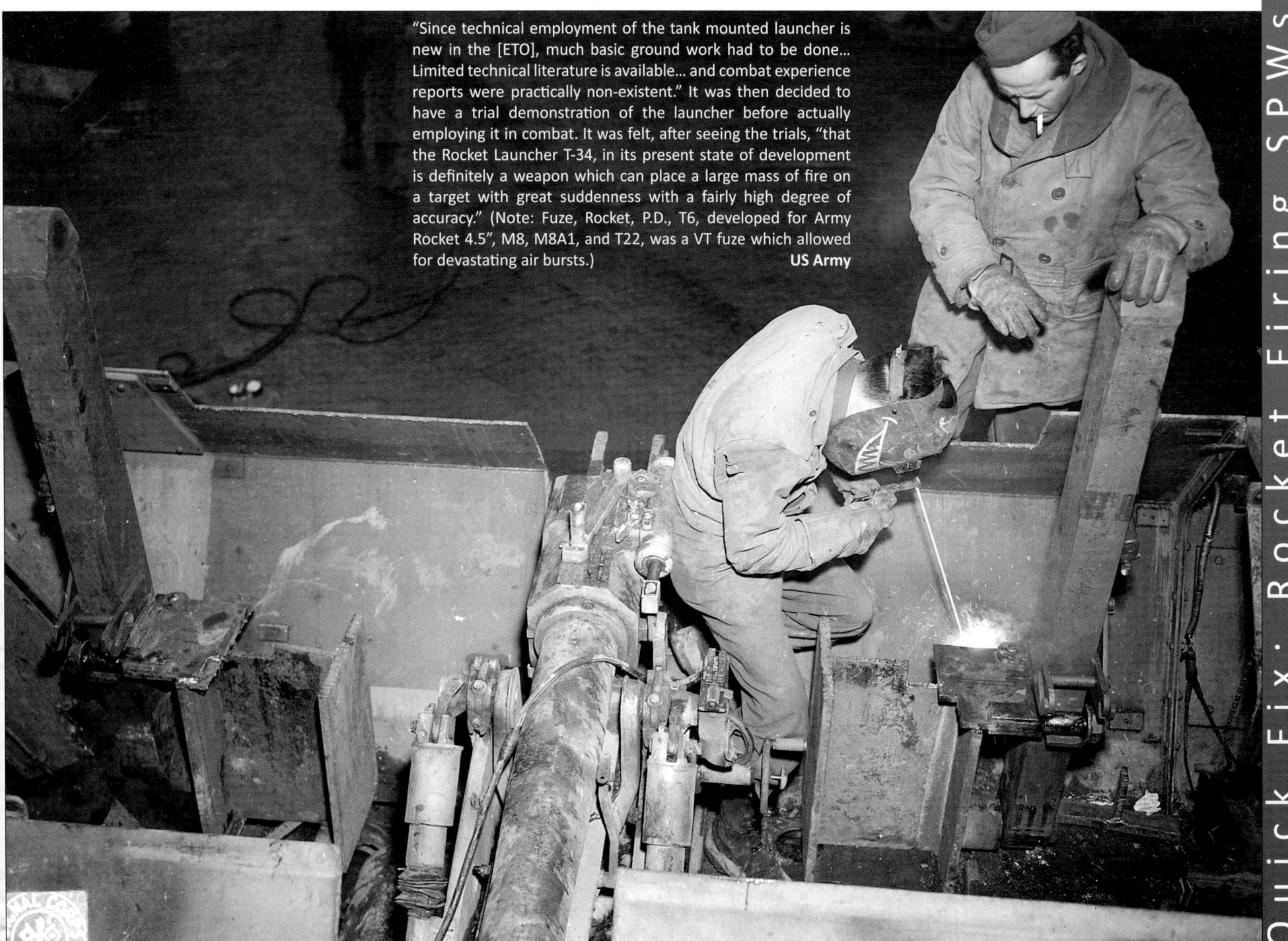

"Since technical employment of the tank mounted launcher is new in the [ETO], much basic ground work had to be done… Limited technical literature is available… and combat experience reports were practically non-existent." It was then decided to have a trial demonstration of the launcher before actually employing it in combat. It was felt, after seeing the trials, "that the Rocket Launcher T-34, in its present state of development is definitely a weapon which can place a large mass of fire on a target with great suddenness with a fairly high degree of accuracy." (Note: Fuze, Rocket, P.D., T6, developed for Army Rocket 4.5", M8, M8A1, and T22, was a VT fuze which allowed for devastating air bursts.) **US Army**

Although the T-34 was a rather massive affair, and each rocket had an effect equal to a 105mm HE shell, just about every component was fragile: The fibre rocket tubes were easily damaged. The tubes, although not the rockets, were materially affected by the weather, and the clamp ring adjustment, too, affected the diameter of the tube. Tubes flaked due to rocket blast. Small fittings worked loose or were easily damaged and electrical connections had to be constantly inspected and repaired. Rocket holding latches were weak (some rockets actually fell out during firing), and contact arms were unsatisfactory. Ripple fire caused the mount to 'lash'.

2x US Army

Above: The driver's compartment with control box installed. The control box contained the timing relays and segment switch. A dial marked 0-60 indicated the firing status of the rockets. Two twelve volt batteries provided current necessary for firing the rockets. (These were later moved outside the compartment to provide more room. An auxiliary generator was carried to ensure maximum voltage to the igniter.) A SCR 509 radio was also installed. Although a rear bulkhead was installed, test firing showed that flames entered the compartment, so all cracks were sealed. Stabilisation of the vehicle was also necessary, so an 8 foot split trail was welded on the left side of the vehicle and the vehicle's springs shimmed. It was desirable to place the left track lower than the right one to ensure maximum elevation. **2x US Army**

Quick Fix: Rocket Firing SPWs

The 'donor' vehicles came from Pz.Brig.108's Pz.Gren.Btl. 2108, which was destroyed in heavy fighting at Bardenberg in October, 1944. Here we have an ex-Sd.Kfz.251/3 with tactical number '2311' and the name 'Heinrich Hötger' painted on the armour. Hötger was a Grenadier, born 10.01.26, who died 21.09.44, the day Pz.Brig.108 and Panzer Lehr-Division attacked the American bridgehead east of Wallendorf in the Eifel. They pushed back the US 5th Armored Division and retook Kruchten and Hommerdingen. Hötger is buried at the cemetery at Neuerburg.

US Army

Quick Fix: Rocket Firing SPWs

Five mittlerer Schützenpanzerwagen have been identified:

Sd.Kfz.251/3: Tact # '2311' and 'Heinrich Hötger' on side armour. 'Shark' insignia on front and rear armour (see page 94). Licence # WH-1713787. Radio aerial in right rear corner of fighting compartment.

SdKfz.251/21: Vehicle had its armour removed while undergoing extensive modification. Radio aerial was located on top right hand corner of 'Zusatzpanzerung'. Travel lock for Drilling still in place.

Sd.Kfz.251/?: Tact # '405', Licence # WH-1749412. Penetration hole in left side armour.

Sd.Kfz.251/?: Licence # WH-1787961. Two penetration holes in right side engine armour, one hole in nose armour.

Sd.Kfz.251/?: Tact # '--32' (armour partially cut away.) 'Shark' insignia on rear armour.

US Army

A view of the mount before firing. After firing, the launcher was examined and found to have 28 of the 60 electrical connections in need of repair. These included twelve broken contact wires, six contact arms out of their hinges, three contact fingers broken, three bent contact arms, and six contact springs disconnected. Two tubes required replacing. These factors indicated it was best, when employing the launcher, to plan to fire only one salvo and then withdraw to the rear area for repairs.

US Army

On 15 December 1944, test firing of the launcher was conducted in the vicinity of Norweiden (more likely Broichweiden), Germany. The launcher was loaded in Kolonie Kellersberg and towed by light tank using a tow bar to the range, a distance of 8.5 miles. (Halftracks were later repaired so that they would run.)

It took approx 20 min to dig the ditch for the track, survey the position, and lay the launcher. The halftracks had to be jockeyed to line up with the aiming stakes as there was no traverse mechanism. The commander used the M1 quadrant to check elevation while the driver elevated or depressed the launcher at his command.

2x US Army

Quick Fix: Rocket Firing SPWs

The halftracks were manned by crews from the HQ Co, 7th Armd Gp although only one mud spattered example was used for the trial. A total of 60 rounds was fired using both single and ripple fire. Note the 'escape' hatch.

US Army

See Michael Eastes, "The 251 Calliope: The Facts Behind an Unusual Vehicle," *Journal of Military Ordnance 8, No.3 (May 1998): 17*, for a first person account by Winston Eastes, a member of 7th Armd Gp who crewed one of these vehicles.

The vehicle rocked excessively and the left track settled during firing, but all rounds hit the target area. The projectile could be heard from the time it left the launcher until it hit and had a low, moaning sound. The flash from the launcher was clearly visible from the target area. On 17 December, the 30th was rushed to the Malmedy-Stavelot sector of Belgium: The Battle of the Bulge was on.

4x US Army

Quick Fix: Rocket Firing SPWs

Why did US forces convert a number of captured m.S.P.W. (Sd.Kfz.251)? What unusual insignia was on them? What does the interior of a Flammpanzer 38 look like? What armoured vehicles were at Meppen? What does a see-through Jagdtiger look like? How can you tell a factory fresh m.S.P.W. (7.5cm Pak) Sd.Kfz.251/22 from a converted m.S.P.W. (7.5cm Kanone) Sd.Kfz.251/9? The answers to these and other questions are to be found here in Panzerwrecks 6, with 119 rare and unpublished large format photographs sourced from around the world.

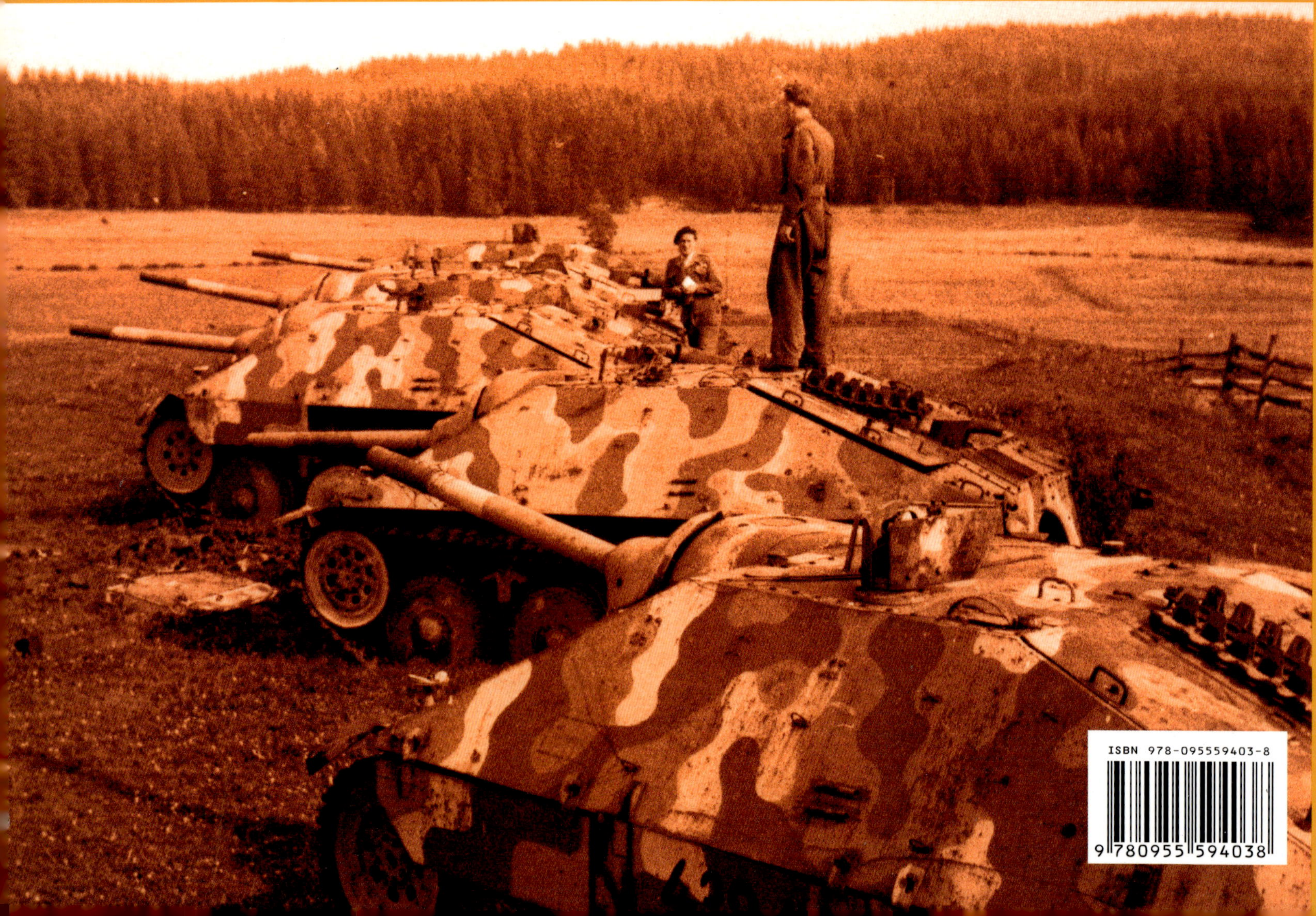

ISBN 978-095559403-8
9 780955 594038

www.panzerwrecks.com

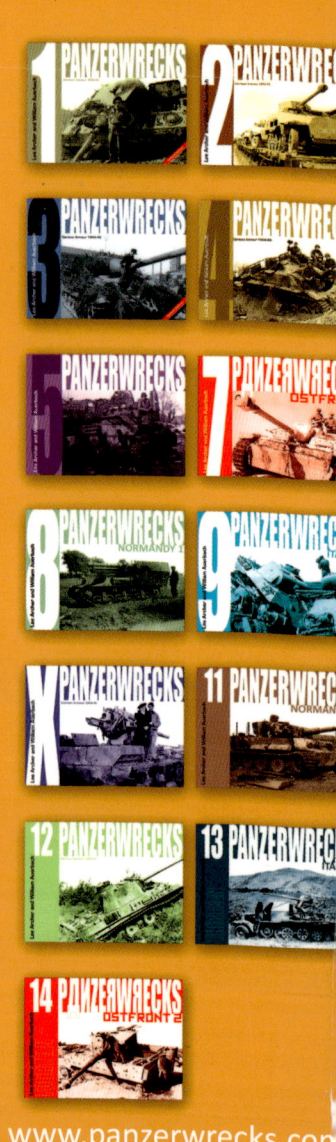